Global Financial Nexus

Navigating the Interbank and OTC Markets

George Andrew

For permission requests, write to the publisher at [musadirri21992@gmail.com].

Table of contents

1.0 Introduction

- Counterparty Risks

- Market Risks

- Regulatory Compliance and Risk Mitigation

6.0 Technology and Innovation

- Fintech Integration

- Automation in Trading Processes

- Impact on Market Efficiency

7.0 Case Studies

- Notable Events in Interbank and OTC Markets

- Lessons Learned and Best Practices

8.0 Future Trends and Emerging Challenges

- Evolving Market Structures

- Technological Advancements

- Regulatory Developments

CHAPTER ONE

1.0 Introduction

The introduction sets the stage for the exploration of the global financial nexus, focusing on the Interbank and Over-The-Counter (OTC) markets.

- **Understanding the Global Financial Landscape:** This section delves into the intricacies of the worldwide financial ecosystem. It examines the interconnectedness of economies, the role of financial institutions, and the dynamics of global markets. Readers will gain insights into the complex web of financial relationships that shape the contemporary economic landscape.

- **Significance of Interbank and OTC Markets:** Here, the focus shifts to why Interbank and OTC markets are pivotal components of the global financial system. It outlines the functions they serve, their historical importance, and their roles in facilitating liquidity and capital flow. This section emphasizes the unique features of these markets and their impact on broader financial stability and economic growth. By the end of the introduction, readers should have a solid foundation for a deeper exploration of these critical financial domains.

CHAPTER TWO

2.0 Foundations of Interbank Market

This chapter delves into the historical evolution, key players, and the array of instruments traded within the Interbank market, providing a comprehensive understanding of its foundational elements.

- **Historical Evolution:** Unraveling the historical roots of the Interbank market, this section traces its development over time. Beginning with its origins and milestones, it explores how the Interbank market evolved in response to changing economic landscapes, technological advancements, and regulatory influences. By examining historical trends, readers gain insights into the market's adaptive nature and its pivotal role in shaping modern financial systems.

- **Key Players and Institutions:** This part identifies and analyzes the major participants that form the backbone of the Interbank market. From central banks to commercial banks and other financial institutions, the chapter highlights their roles, interactions, and the mechanisms through which they contribute to market liquidity and stability. Understanding the key players provides a nuanced perspective on the intricate relationships that define the Interbank market.

- **Instruments Traded in Interbank Market:** The chapter explores the diverse range of financial instruments actively traded within the Interbank market. This includes various money market instruments, such as interbank loans, certificates of deposit, and commercial paper. Additionally, it delves into the trading of financial derivatives like interest rate swaps and forward rate agreements. By elucidating the instruments, their functions, and the risk management strategies associated with them, readers gain a comprehensive grasp of the financial instruments that drive Interbank market transactions. This foundational knowledge sets the stage for more in-depth explorations into the intricacies of this crucial financial domain.

CHAPTER THREE

3.0 Over-The-Counter (OTC) Market Dynamics

This chapter provides a detailed exploration of the Over-The-Counter (OTC) market, focusing on its structure, the diversity of products traded, and the regulatory framework governing its operations.

- Overview and Structure: This section offers a comprehensive overview of the OTC market, highlighting its decentralized nature and the absence of a centralized exchange. Readers gain insights into the direct dealings between buyers and sellers, characterized by negotiated transactions.

The chapter examines how this structure influences the market's flexibility, allowing for tailored transactions that may not be feasible on traditional exchanges. Understanding the dynamics of OTC market structure lays the foundation for comprehending its unique features and challenges.

- **Products and Participants:** The chapter explores the wide array of financial products traded over the counter. From bonds and derivatives to commodities and structured products, readers gain an understanding of the diversity and complexity of OTC instruments. Additionally, it outlines the various participants involved, including institutional investors, banks, corporations, and individual traders. Examining the roles and motivations of these participants provides valuable insights into the OTC market's vibrancy and its significance in meeting the diverse financial needs of market participants.

- **Regulatory Framework:** Delving into the regulatory landscape, this section outlines the rules and frameworks governing OTC markets. It explores the measures implemented to enhance transparency, mitigate risks, and ensure fair and efficient operations. This includes an analysis of regulatory bodies, reporting requirements, and the evolving global regulatory landscape. Understanding the regulatory framework is crucial for readers to grasp the mechanisms in place to maintain market integrity and protect participants. As regulatory dynamics play a pivotal role in shaping the OTC market, this section sets the stage for discussions on compliance and the evolving nature of financial regulations.

CHAPTER FOUR

4.0 Market Interactions and Influencing Factors

This chapter delves into the intricate web of interactions and the multifaceted factors that shape the dynamics of global financial markets.

- **Interconnectedness of Global Markets:** Examining the interconnected nature of global markets, this section elucidates how events in one part of the world can have ripple effects across financial markets. It explores the interdependence of economies, financial institutions, and markets, highlighting the transmission mechanisms that propagate shocks and influences globally. Understanding market interconnectedness is crucial for investors, policymakers, and market participants as they navigate the complexities of a highly integrated and interlinked global financial system.

- **Economic Indicators and Market Trends:** This part explores the symbiotic relationship between economic indicators and market trends. It delves into how key economic indicators, such as GDP growth, inflation rates, and employment figures, serve as vital benchmarks for assessing market conditions. Readers gain insights into how market trends emerge in response to these indicators, influencing investment decisions, market sentiment, and risk perceptions. Analyzing this relationship equips readers with the tools to interpret market movements and make informed decisions in response to economic signals.

- **Geopolitical Influences:** The chapter investigates the impact of geopolitical events on financial markets. Geopolitical factors, such as international conflicts, trade tensions, and diplomatic developments, can significantly influence market behavior. This section explores how geopolitical risks create uncertainties and affect investor confidence, leading to market fluctuations. Understanding these influences is crucial for anticipating potential market disruptions and developing strategies to manage geopolitical risks effectively.

By exploring these interconnected elements, readers gain a holistic understanding of the intricate factors that drive market interactions and influence global financial dynamics. This knowledge is essential for market participants seeking to navigate the uncertainties inherent in the constantly evolving landscape of international finance.

CHAPTER FIVE

5.0 Risk Management in Global Markets

This chapter focuses on the critical aspect of risk management in the context of global markets, addressing specific risks and strategies for mitigating them.

- **Counterparty Risks:** Exploring the realm of counterparty risks, this section delves into the challenges associated with potential default by a trading partner. It examines the importance of assessing the creditworthiness and reliability of counterparties in financial transactions, especially in markets where participants engage in complex financial instruments. Strategies such as collateralization, credit risk analysis, and the use of derivative instruments for hedging are discussed to illustrate how market participants navigate and mitigate counterparty risks.

- **Market Risks:** This part delves into the various market risks that participants face in global financial markets. It encompasses price fluctuations, interest rate changes, currency fluctuations, and other factors that can impact the value of financial instruments. Readers gain insights into risk assessment methodologies, including value-at-risk (VaR) models, stress testing, and scenario analysis. Understanding market risks is crucial for developing risk management strategies, employing hedging techniques, and making informed investment decisions in dynamic market conditions.

- Regulatory Compliance and Risk Mitigation: The chapter explores the regulatory landscape and its role in risk management. It discusses the importance of regulatory compliance in mitigating systemic risks and maintaining market integrity. This includes an examination of risk management standards set by regulatory bodies, reporting requirements, and the evolving regulatory environment. By understanding regulatory frameworks, market participants can implement effective risk mitigation strategies that align with compliance standards.

By providing a comprehensive view of counterparty risks, market risks, and regulatory considerations, this chapter equips readers with the knowledge needed to navigate the complexities of risk management in global markets. It emphasizes the proactive measures and strategies employed by market participants to safeguard against potential pitfalls and uncertainties inherent in the international financial landscape.

CHAPTER SIX

6.0 Technology and Innovation

This chapter delves into the transformative role of technology and innovation in the global financial landscape, with a specific focus on Fintech integration, automation in trading processes, and their collective impact on market efficiency.

- Fintech Integration: Exploring the intersection of finance and technology, this section examines the growing influence of Fintech solutions in reshaping traditional financial practices. It covers areas such as digital banking, blockchain technology, robo-advisors, and mobile payment systems. Readers gain insights into how Fintech integration enhances accessibility, efficiency, and user experience, disrupting conventional financial models and creating new avenues for market participation.

- **Automation in Trading Processes:** The chapter delves into the increasing prevalence of automation in trading, with algorithmic trading and high-frequency trading playing pivotal roles. It explores how sophisticated algorithms and automated trading systems execute trades at high speeds, responding to market conditions in real-time. This section discusses the benefits of automation, including reduced transaction costs, enhanced liquidity, and improved market liquidity. However, it also addresses associated challenges such as algorithmic risks and the potential for market disruptions.

- **Impact on Market Efficiency:** Examining the broader implications, this part assesses how technology and innovation contribute to overall market efficiency. It explores how automation and

Fintech solutions can streamline processes, reduce transaction times, and enhance information dissemination. Additionally, it discusses the challenges of maintaining market integrity and fairness in an environment where technology plays a dominant role. Understanding the impact on market efficiency is crucial for market participants, regulators, and policymakers as they navigate the evolving landscape shaped by technological advancements.

By providing an in-depth exploration of Fintech integration, automation in trading processes, and their influence on market efficiency, this chapter equips readers with a nuanced understanding of the transformative forces at play in the contemporary global financial ecosystem. It emphasizes the need for adaptability and strategic considerations in an environment where technology continually reshapes the dynamics of financial markets.

CHAPTER SEVEN

7.0 Case Studies

This chapter delves into real-world scenarios, examining notable events in both the Interbank and Over-The-Counter (OTC) markets. The analysis goes beyond theory, providing practical insights into the dynamics and outcomes of key events.

- **Notable Events in Interbank and OTC Markets:** This section presents case studies of significant occurrences in the Interbank and OTC markets. It could include events such as financial crises, market disruptions, or instances of successful risk management strategies. By dissecting these events, readers gain a deeper understanding of the complexities and challenges inherent in global financial markets. The case studies serve as real-life examples, illustrating the impact of decisions made by market participants, regulatory responses, and the broader implications for the financial system.

Examples of a case studies

In the ever-evolving landscape of global finance, the interconnected web of markets, institutions, and participants forms a complex nexus. This case study explores a pivotal period marked by significant events, demonstrating the intricate dynamics and challenges within the global financial nexus.

Background:

Amidst a backdrop of economic globalization, rapid technological advancements, and shifting geopolitical tides, the financial world faced unprecedented challenges and opportunities. The period under consideration spans from 2019 to 2021, encapsulating the COVID-19 pandemic, volatile market conditions, and transformative trends in financial technology.

Events:

1. COVID-19 Pandemic Shock (2020): The outbreak of the COVID-19 pandemic triggered widespread market disruptions. Volatility soared as uncertainties surrounding the economic impact of lockdowns and the effectiveness of policy responses unfolded. Central banks implemented unprecedented monetary measures, influencing interest rates and liquidity in the Interbank market.

2. Rise of Fintech Innovations (2019-2021): During this period, Fintech integration accelerated, impacting both Interbank and Over-The-Counter (OTC) markets. Blockchain applications gained traction, and algorithmic trading systems became more sophisticated. The integration of Fintech brought efficiencies but also raised questions about regulatory frameworks and the resilience of automated systems.

3. Geopolitical Trade Tensions (2019-2020): Geopolitical events, particularly trade tensions between major economies, introduced uncertainties into the global financial nexus. Fluctuations in currency values and commodity prices underscored the interconnectedness of markets and the influence of geopolitical developments on investor sentiment.

Lessons Learned:

1. Adaptive Risk Management: Institutions that successfully weathered the storm demonstrated adept risk management strategies. The ability to swiftly adapt risk frameworks, assess counterparty risks, and implement hedging techniques proved crucial in navigating market uncertainties.

2. Resilience Through Technology: Firms embracing technological advancements, including cloud-based infrastructure and data analytics, exhibited resilience. However, the increased reliance on technology also highlighted the importance of cybersecurity measures and regulatory compliance.

3. Regulatory Agility: Regulatory bodies played a pivotal role in shaping the response to emerging challenges. The case study underscores the need for regulatory frameworks to adapt swiftly to technological advancements and evolving market structures to maintain market integrity and investor protection.

Looking Ahead:

As the case study concludes, it provides a glimpse into the future of the global financial nexus. Anticipated trends include further integration of sustainable finance practices, advancements in artificial intelligence impacting decision-making processes, and continued efforts to enhance cybersecurity in the financial industry.

Conclusion:

The case study of the global financial nexus during this pivotal period illustrates the resilience, challenges, and transformative nature of the interconnected financial landscape. By dissecting these events and drawing lessons, market participants can better prepare for the uncertainties and opportunities that lie ahead in the dynamic world of global finance.

- Lessons Learned and Best Practices: Building on the analysis of case studies, this part distills lessons learned and identifies best practices. It explores how market participants, institutions, and regulators adapted to challenges and seized opportunities. By examining successful strategies and analyzing shortcomings, readers gain actionable insights applicable to their own decision-making processes. The chapter aims to provide a valuable resource for individuals and organizations seeking to enhance their understanding of risk management, market dynamics, and strategic decision-making in the context of Interbank and OTC markets.

Case studies offer a bridge between theoretical concepts and practical application, allowing readers to draw connections between theory and real-world scenarios. By studying the experiences of others, market participants can better navigate uncertainties and develop informed strategies for their own engagement in the dynamic landscape of global financial markets.

CHAPTER EIGHT

8.0 Future Trends and Emerging Challenges

This chapter anticipates the trajectory of global financial markets, exploring future trends and the challenges that may arise. It focuses on three key aspects: evolving market structures, technological advancements, and regulatory developments.

- **Evolving Market Structures:** This section analyzes the shifts in market structures, including changes in trading venues, the emergence of new financial products, and the evolution of participant roles. It explores how factors such as globalization, demographic trends, and market innovation contribute to reshaping the dynamics of financial markets. Understanding evolving market structures is essential for market participants to anticipate changes in liquidity, trading patterns, and the overall functioning of financial ecosystems.

- **Technological Advancements:** The chapter delves into the continuing impact of technological advancements on global financial markets. It examines how technologies such as artificial intelligence, distributed ledger technology, and quantum computing are likely to influence market operations. Discussions may revolve around the potential benefits, risks, and ethical considerations associated with the increasing integration of cutting-edge technologies. A nuanced understanding of technological advancements is crucial for market participants to stay competitive and adapt to the evolving landscape of financial services.

- **Regulatory Developments:** This part explores the evolving regulatory landscape and its implications for global financial markets. It considers regulatory responses to emerging risks, changes in compliance standards, and international cooperation in regulatory frameworks. Analyzing regulatory developments is vital for market participants to navigate the evolving compliance landscape and understand how regulatory changes may impact market dynamics and their own operational processes.

By examining future trends and emerging challenges in evolving market structures, technological advancements, and regulatory developments, this chapter equips readers with foresight into the potential directions of global financial markets. Anticipating these trends and challenges is essential for informed decision-making, risk management, and strategic planning in an environment characterized by continual change and innovation.

CHAPTER NINE

9.0 Strategic Decision-Making in a Globalized Context

This chapter focuses on the key components of strategic decision-making in the globalized context of financial markets, addressing investment strategies, hedging techniques, and the ability to adapt to changing market conditions.

- **Investment Strategies:** This section explores various investment strategies employed by market participants in the global context. It encompasses considerations such as asset allocation, portfolio diversification, and investment styles ranging from value investing to growth strategies. The chapter provides insights into the factors influencing investment decisions, including market trends, economic indicators, and risk tolerance. Understanding different investment strategies is crucial for individuals and institutions seeking to optimize returns and manage risks in a globally interconnected financial landscape.

- **Hedging Techniques:** The chapter delves into the importance of hedging as a risk management strategy in the face of market uncertainties. It explores various hedging techniques, including the use of derivatives such as options and futures contracts. Readers gain insights into how market participants use hedging to protect against adverse price movements, currency fluctuations, and other risks inherent in global markets. The section emphasizes the role of hedging in preserving capital and enhancing overall portfolio stability.

- Adapting to Changing Market Conditions: Recognizing the dynamic nature of global financial markets, this part emphasizes the necessity of adaptability. It explores how successful market participants continually reassess and adjust their strategies in response to changing economic conditions, geopolitical events, and technological advancements. Strategies for staying agile, such as ongoing education, monitoring market trends, and leveraging advanced analytics, are discussed. Adapting to changing market conditions is crucial for sustained success and resilience in a globalized financial environment.

By addressing strategic decision-making in the globalized context through investment strategies, hedging techniques, and adaptability to changing market conditions, this chapter equips readers with the knowledge and tools needed to navigate the complexities of international finance. It underscores the importance of a proactive and flexible approach in achieving long-term financial objectives in a world characterized by rapid change and interconnected markets.

CHAPTER TEN

10.0 Conclusion

The concluding chapter provides a summary of key insights gleaned throughout the exploration of global financial markets, concluding with a forward-looking perspective on the future of these markets.

- **Recap of Key Insights:** This section synthesizes the crucial takeaways from the preceding chapters. It recaps fundamental concepts, pivotal events, and strategic considerations discussed in the book. The recap serves as a reminder of the foundational knowledge presented, reinforcing the reader's understanding of the complexities and dynamics of global financial markets.

- **Looking Ahead: The Future of Global Financial Markets**: The chapter concludes by peering into the future of global financial markets. It explores potential trends, challenges, and opportunities that may shape the landscape. This forward-looking perspective may touch on themes such as sustainability, evolving technologies, geopolitical shifts, and regulatory developments.

By considering the trajectory of global financial markets, the conclusion provides readers with a framework for continued learning and adaptation in the ever-changing world of international finance.

In essence, the conclusion ties together the various threads explored throughout the book, offering a comprehensive understanding of global financial markets. It acts as a springboard for readers to apply their knowledge in navigating the current landscape and prepares them for the ongoing evolution of global financial markets in the years to come.

Anticipate more publications on this, thanks.